the art of letting go.

Bernadette Anne Paz

BookLeaf Publishing

Presentation by *BookLeaf Publishing*

Web: www.bookleafpub.com

E-mail: info@bookleafpub.com

ISBN: 978-93-95950-37-4

First edition 2022

I

I love you.
There, I finally said it.
And now,
it's time for me to
admit something else.
I have to let you go
because although it has
taken me a while,
I am slowly
coming to the realisation
that maybe
I am in love with the
idea and version of you
that I created in my head.
The fruit of my imagination
that I planted using
the way you made me feel
safe, carefree and that somehow
the world is at my fingertips
and that I can achieve everything.
The way your
smile, laugh and presence
made me look forward to seeing you.
How you made me feel
everything and nothing at the same time.

So I guess
this is my thank you
and my farewell,
for the happiness, the time you gave me
and the adventures we shared.

II

So this is how it ends.
Two souls
in the same city
so close
yet,
I have never felt
as great a distance
like the one we have now.

III

Our fragile hearts
felt so much Love
but Fate has its own way.
Deep inside
we knew that we couldn't be more but
In between our conversations,
jokes and petty little fights,
You asked me
"Will you be there until end?"
And without missing a beat,
I answered you
"Always".

IV

5

Fated hearts, distant lives.
Like parallel lines we always get close
but never become together.
Our souls always wandering,
Wondering when it will be.
That promised day,
Our infinity.

V

I still remember the first time I saw you.
I had tired eyes, messy hair
And a temper that was decimated as if on cue.
You walked towards where I was,
A shy smile on your face.
All I could think of was
"Oh god, this one will be worth the heartbreak"

VI

"I'm selfish, I don't like sharing"
These were the words I uttered trying to show
you my horrible side.
"What's mine is mine and i'll fight whoever
takes it away from me"
I continued on trying to see how you'll react.
I braced myself for the worst,
For you to turn away and run for the hills.
Instead you laughed onto the sea,
Faced me and took my hand.
"That's okay, I'm a jealous person. I don't like
sharing as well."
And with that the wind carried away my worries,
settling my chaotic thoughts.

VII

How can you forget someone who gave you so
much to remember?
We spent so many days and nights
Talking, laughing
and telling each other our vulnerabilities.
We came to know what pushes each other's
buttons
But still, who would have known?
That a day will come
where we are only known to each other as
Strangers who share so much memories.
I tried to hold on to what was left of us
But i couldn't force it.
It slipped right through my hands
And we had to go our separate ways.

VIII

For many seasons
I let the seeds of this love grow.
Diligently watering
and keeping it close to my heart.
People kept on asking
"Why do you bother? The flowers aren't even
blooming"
Despite their doubt, i kept going.
Until one summer the flowers bloomed
But it grew somewhere else.
Some place where it was free,
Where it could grow wild and carefree.
It created a storm within me
Breaking down the walls that kept me sane.
One after the other,the lightning struck and
brought me to my knees.
Shedding tears and clutching the brokenness left,
i looked up and asked why.
The wind roared and I felt the warmth settle
within me.
I found peace at the heart of the storm

IX

I guess it's Fate's cruel joke.
You're always within my reach
But i can never get to you.
It haunts me at night
Keeping me restless and awake.
I'm trying to run away from it
But it keeps on pulling me back.
To the place where i keep on drowning
And asking you to hold my hand.
I'm trying to make sense of it all
But it's driving me to the edge.
Until when are you going to keep this up?
Set me free or take my hand.

X

A few years ago, i fell apart
and i haven't been the same since.
I've travelled places after places
to try and find the familiar feeling of home
Yet the further I went,
the more confused I became.
One day i went back to place where I first
started and there I found it.
The person I should have loved first,
Myself.

XI

I love you but i can't keep breaking my heart
over and over again for someone who's not even
willing to give "us" a try.
Here I am willing to risk everything for you
and there you are, saying you're willing to risk
things for me but not even sure as to what.
Darling, i'm not asking you to.
I can't force you to or make you risk things for
me.
You have to do them willingly because I want a
love that comes from the bottom of your heart.
I want a love that I know you won't have to
force yourself to do or risk things because you
feel obligated to.
I want it to be sincere.

XII

I had this future planned out with you inside my
head.
All the important milestones that I wanted to
share with you until the end.
Most nights I played them out like a movie
I was so sure of you
But in the end,
none of it became true.
All I had was myself.
I broke free from the heartbreak.
I worked on myself, my dreams
And like a phoenix, i rose up from the ashes.

XIII

Whenever I used to get cold, i'd reach out to you
and wrap myself in your arms.
My comfort and my safe haven.
You protected me from my nightmares, from the
darkness that haunted me.
You were the knight that helped me fight the
dragons in my sleep and the reassuring smile
that fought off my demons when everything was
falling apart.
Yet on that one stormy night, i woke up with a
gasp and tried to reach out but you have
disappeared.
The demons and dragons won.
The darkness seeped in and the nightmares took
over
You took my comfort, my safe haven.
Now i wrap myself in my own arms, reaching
out to no one and learning to stand up to the cold

XIV

I keep scrolling through social media just so I
can keep up to date with what is happening with
everyone's lives.
In the midst of it all, it dawned on me.
Although i'm not yet living the full life I have
dreamt for myself,
I am living a life I worked so hard for.
It made me appreciate the everyday battles I
faced, what I have and who is still around.
I will get there one day but for now,
All I need to do is live in the present.

XV

Dear You
I must admit for a good few years of my life,
You were my everything.
You gave me the bare minimum yet it made me
so happy.
You gave me a few minutes of your time yet I
was so elated.
Thinking back, I cannot even believe the
excuses I gave myself for reassurance.
Now I have realised the truth.
You exploited my love for you.
You used my naivety to your advantage.
But still, thank you for the happy memories.
I hope nothing but the best for you.
I hope you become a better person for the future
And last but not the least, I hope karma gets you.

XVI

I am still healing.
I had so much love to give to people who could
not love me back.
I am trying to find peace yet,
I can still feel the pain and anger in me.
Slowly, ever so slowly
I can feel myself becoming whole again.
When the time comes,
I will be unstoppable.

XVII

It's always so hard describing who I am
But this is how I can describe myself.
I am a product of my parent's dreams.
I am the daughter of immigrants who flew
across the ocean in the hopes of a better life.
They took a gamble in life to make sure that I
have the opportunities that they were not given
in their early years.
Although my life has not turned out the way
they or I expected it to be, I will forever be
thankful to them.
For my life, my sister and their never ending
sacrifices.

XVIII

It took me a while to get there but
I can finally say it —
I do not need somebody else's love.
I am happy.
I am content.
I am and will always be enough.